DISCARD

Moose

by Lesley A. DuTemple
photographs by Frank Staub

Lerner Publications Company • Minneapolis, Minnesota

*For little Margaret love-love—my daughter, my friend, and a
great moose-watching companion*

—LAD

To Ken, Cindy, Alicia, Daniel, and Jonathan
—FS

*Thanks to our series consultant, Sharyn Fenwick, elementary science/math specialist. Mrs.
Fenwick was the winner of the National Science Teachers Association 1991 Distinguished
Teaching Award. She also was the recipient of the Presidential Award for Excellence in Math and
Science Teaching, representing the state of Minnesota at the elementary level in 1992.*

*Additional photographs are reproduced through the courtesy of: pp. 6, 11, 20, 25, 30, 39, 40
© Beth Davidow.*

Early Bird Nature Books were conceptualized
by Ruth Berman and designed by Steve Foley.
Series editor is Joelle Goldman.

Website address: www.lernerbooks.com

Library of Congress Cataloging-in-Publication Data

DuTemple, Lesley A.
    Moose / by Lesley A. DuTemple : photographs by Frank Staub.
      p.   cm. — (Early bird nature books)
    Includes index.
    Summary: Describes the physical characteristics, habitat, and
behavior of moose.
    ISBN 0-8225-3031-7 (alk. paper)
    1. Moose—Juvenile literature. [1. Moose.] I. Staub, Frank J.,
ill. II. Title. III. Series.
    QL737.U55D88 1998
    599.65'7—dc21   97-24685

Manufactured in the United States of America
1 2 3 4 5 6 – JR – 03 02 01 00 99 98

Contents

Moose live in North America and in parts of Europe and Asia. The striped area shows where moose live in North America.

Be a Word Detective

Can you find these words as you read about the moose's life? Be a detective and try to figure out what they mean. You can turn to the glossary on page 46 for help.

antlers	cows	predators
bell	habitat	ruminants
bull	herbivores	rut
calves	hooves	velvet
cast	pedicle	

Chapter 1

The moose's scientific name is Alces alces. Where do moose live?

The Biggest Deer in the World

In the north woods, winters are long and cold. The snow is so deep, it would be over your head. The temperature is below freezing for weeks at a time. In summer, the ground is wet and swampy. Swarms of biting insects fill the air. This is where moose live.

Moose are members of the deer family.
There are many kinds of deer in the world.
Deer have lived on earth for millions of years.

This moose is looking for food.

Moose are the biggest deer in the world. They are more than 6 feet tall. That is taller than most people. And moose weigh 800 to 1,400 pounds. Just one moose could weigh more than 20 children. One large moose could weigh as much as all the children in your class.

The moose is one of the largest animals in North America. Only bison and Alaskan brown bears grow bigger than moose.

About one million moose live in North America.

Millions of years ago, moose were small. Scientists have found very old moose skeletons. These skeletons show that long ago, moose were no bigger than a house cat! But over millions of years, moose got bigger and bigger.

Chapter 2

This moose is standing in a marshy area. What are some other places where moose live?

Life in the North Woods

Moose live in northern and western North America and in parts of Europe and Asia. They live in forests, marshes, and ponds. These places are the best moose habitat. A habitat is a place where a certain kind of animal can live. Moose habitat has to have leafy trees and freshwater. It also has to have cold weather.

Moose have long, skinny legs. In winter, a moose's long legs help it move through deep snow. Moose can even run in deep snow.

Snow helps moose stay warm. When it's snowing hard, a moose lies down and makes a bed in the snow. The snow bed protects the moose from cold winds.

Some kinds of deer live in large groups. But moose usually live alone.

Moose have big shoulders that form a hump.

Moose have thick, shaggy fur. Each hair in the fur is hollow. Hollow hairs trap air next to a moose's body. This helps the moose stay warm. Hollow hairs also help the moose float. Moose are great swimmers.

A moose's wide feet are called hooves.
Each hoof is split into two toes. In summer,
moose spend a lot of time wading in marshes
and ponds. When a moose walks in a wet area,
the toes on its hooves spread apart. This keeps
the moose from sinking or getting stuck.

This is a moose's footprint. You can see the marks made by the moose's two toes.

Chapter 3

Moose eat only plants. What are animals who eat plants called?

Leaves for Lunch

Moose are herbivores (HUR-buh-vorz). A herbivore is an animal who eats only plants. Plants are hard to digest (dye-JEST). That means it's hard for a moose's body to change plants so it can use them as food. But moose are also ruminants (ROO-muh-nuhnts). Moose and many other ruminants have four stomachs. They use their extra stomachs to help them digest the plants they eat.

Moose eat the tender twigs of willows and other trees. Moose also eat shrubs. Shrubs are plants with woody stems that grow near the ground.

Moose eat woody plants. This moose is kneeling down to eat food that is on the ground.

Moose don't bite leaves off trees. They tear them off. A moose has no upper teeth in the front of its mouth. It has only lower teeth in front. But a moose has a strong upper lip. A moose uses its upper lip to grab leaves and young branches. Then it presses its upper lip against its bottom teeth and rips the leaves off.

A moose can eat about 20,000 leaves in one day.

Sometimes a moose pulls all the leaves off a branch at once.

Sometimes a moose grabs a branch and pulls it sideways through its mouth. That strips all the leaves off at once. It gives the moose a big mouthful of leaves to chew.

A moose looks for underwater plants. Moose need to eat both water plants and land plants.

Besides twigs and leaves, moose eat pond plants. In summer, moose spend a lot of time with their heads underwater. They put their heads underwater to get a mouthful of the plants growing on the bottom of the pond. They usually lift their heads out of the water to chew.

Moose eat a lot of plants. In summer, an adult moose eats about 60 pounds of leaves and pond plants every day. That's like eating 60 heads of lettuce.

On a summer day, a moose can eat more than 1,000 pond plants.

In winter, moose have a hard time finding enough food to eat. This moose is eating spruce branches.

In summer, moose can usually find enough to eat. But in winter, it's hard for moose to find enough food. In winter, there are no leaves to eat. So moose have to eat tree bark and tough, older branches. They even eat pine needles. But these foods don't keep moose strong and healthy. Moose lose a lot of weight every winter. Some moose starve to death.

Chapter 4

The male moose grows bigger antlers than any other kind of deer. What is a male moose called?

Velvet to Bone

Deer are the only animals that grow antlers. Female moose don't grow antlers, but males do. A male moose is called a bull. Bull moose grow the biggest antlers of all deer.

Antlers grow from the top of a bull's head. An antler starts to grow from a spot called the pedicle (PEH-dih-kuhl). A bull moose has two pedicles. At first, the pedicles are just fuzzy bumps. But they keep growing all spring and summer. Finally, the antlers are fully grown.

Young moose have small antlers.

Strips of velvet are hanging from this moose's antlers.

Growing antlers are covered with soft, furry skin. This skin is called velvet. Velvet protects the antlers and helps them grow. As the antlers get bigger, the velvet starts to shed, or come off.

A moose's antlers itch when the velvet starts to shed. A moose has rubbed his itchy antlers against this tree. He has scratched off some of the tree's bark.

A bull moose's antlers are bone, like the bones in your body. Antlers are very heavy. They weigh 60 to 85 pounds. Carrying moose antlers on your head would feel as heavy as carrying two bicycles on your head.

For a few months every autumn, bull moose get really cranky. They charge at anything that gets in their way. They even charge each other. And they use their antlers to fight other bulls. The time of autumn when bull moose fight is called the rut.

In the autumn, male moose use their antlers to fight each other.

When the rut is finished, a moose's antlers are cast. When antlers are cast, they fall off. Every spring, a bull grows a new set of antlers. Each year, the antlers grow back bigger than the year before. Young bulls have small antlers. But an older bull might have antlers that are 5 feet across.

This young moose has lost one of his antlers.

Moose can swim 15 miles without stopping.

By winter, most bull moose have cast their antlers. But you won't find many on the ground. Mice and other creatures eat them. Antlers are a healthy food for forest creatures.

Chapter 5

A female moose is called a cow. What is a baby moose called?

Moose Families

Moose usually live alone. Only female moose and their babies live together. Female moose are called cows. Baby moose are called calves.

Moose calves are born in the spring. The weather is warm then. And there's plenty of food for moose to eat. Sometimes moose cows have twins. But usually cows have just one calf at a time.

A baby moose has light brown fur. Its parents' fur is darker brown.

A young moose drinks its mother's milk.

When a moose calf is born, it weighs about 35 pounds. That's about as much as a medium-sized dog. At first, a calf only nurses, or drinks its mother's milk. Calves nurse for several months. But when they're a few weeks old, they start eating plants too. By autumn, a calf eats only plants. By then, a calf may weigh 400 pounds.

A calf doesn't look just like its parents. Adult moose have very dark fur. The fur on their backs looks almost black. But a calf's fur is light brown. Also, an adult moose has a bell. A bell is a flap of furry skin that hangs from a moose's throat. A calf doesn't have a bell. As a calf gets older, it grows one.

The bell is a flap of furry skin that hangs from a moose's throat. A bell can grow to be 20 inches long.

Moose cows take good care of their calves. They stay close and guard their calves from predators (PREH-duh-turz). A predator is an animal that hunts and eats other animals. Wolves and bears are predators who often hunt moose.

A young moose lives with its mother for about one year.

Wolves hunt moose. But usually they can catch only moose that are very young, very old, or very sick.

If a predator comes near, the cow rears up. She kicks the attacker with her front hooves. A moose can kill a predator by kicking with its hooves.

A young moose needs its mother to protect it and feed it.

A newborn calf can't protect itself from predators. A very young calf can't run or swim. But if a calf lives to be one month old, it will probably grow up to become an adult.

By the time a calf is one month old, it can run and swim. It can run into the water and swim away from predators. If a calf gets tired while swimming, it rests its head or front legs on the cow's back. Its mother gives the calf a ride.

Insects sometimes bite moose. When moose go into the water, they don't get bitten as much.

A calf stays with its mother for about a year. Its mother teaches it to find food. She helps it survive the winter. In the spring, when the young moose is about one year old, it leaves its mother. It starts life on its own.

When a moose is about one year old, it can live on its own.

Chapter 6

Bears sometimes hunt moose. Is it easy for a bear to catch a moose?

Dangers and Enemies

 Few predators hunt healthy adult moose. Wolves and bears do hunt moose. But it's hard for them to catch a healthy moose.

A moose can hear and smell its enemies, even when they're far away.

Moose can't see very well. But they have a good sense of smell and hearing. A moose's long nose can smell predators from 1 mile away. And a moose's ears can turn in any direction. A moose can even turn one ear toward the pond and the other toward the forest. When a moose smells or hears a predator, it can run away. Or it can rear up and kick the attacker.

But even a healthy moose can be caught by wolves if it gets stuck in deep snow. Sometimes the top of the snow is solid enough for a wolf to run on, but not solid enough for a moose. The moose sinks through the snow and gets stuck. Then wolves can catch it. But usually, predators only catch calves, old moose, or sick moose.

This moose is standing in knee-deep snow. A moose can't run fast in deep snow.

Sickness can be a problem for moose. Sometimes a moose gets infected by worms or small insects. Then it may get sick and die.

But the biggest danger for moose is dying of hunger in the winter. More moose die from hunger than anything else.

In winter, it's hard for a moose to find enough food to eat.

If too many people move into an area where moose live, the moose usually leave.

Moose usually stay away from people. If people move into moose habitat, the moose usually move out. Sometimes people cut down too many trees in moose habitat. Then the moose have nothing to eat.

People once hunted moose a lot. Many moose were killed. But some states have made laws to protect moose from hunters.

Many moose are hit by cars each year.

People can help protect moose. Then
moose will be in the northern forests and
marshes for a long time to come.

A moose calf eats leaves near a road in Alaska.

On Sharing a Book

As you know, adults greatly influence a child's attitude toward reading. When a child sees you read, or when you share a book with a child, you're sending a message that reading is important. Show the child that reading a book together is important to you. Find a comfortable, quiet place. Turn off the television and limit other distractions, such as telephone calls.

Be prepared to start slowly. Take turns reading parts of this book. Stop and talk about what you're reading. Talk about the photographs. You may find that much of the shared time is spent discussing just a few pages. This discussion time is valuable for both of you, so don't move through the book too quickly. If the child begins to lose interest, stop reading. Continue sharing the book at another time. When you do pick up the book again, be sure to revisit the parts you have already read. Most importantly, enjoy the book!

Be a Vocabulary Detective

You will find a word list on page 5. Words selected for this list are important to the understanding of the topic of this book. Encourage the child to be a word detective and search for the words as you read the book together. Talk about what the words mean and how they are used in the sentence. Do any of these words have more than one meaning? You will find these words defined in a glossary on page 46.

What about Questions?

Use questions to make sure the child understands the information in this book. Here are some suggestions:

> What did this paragraph tell us? What does this picture show? What do you think we'll learn about next? Could a moose live in your backyard? Why/Why not? What would you need to live where moose live? How do moose protect themselves from the cold? How does a moose eat leaves? How is a moose family like your family and how is it different? What do you think it's like being a moose? What is your favorite part of the book? Why?

If the child has questions, don't hesitate to respond with questions of your own, such as: What do *you* think? Why? What is it that you don't know? If the child can't remember certain facts, turn to the index.

Introducing the Index

The index is an important learning tool. It helps readers get information quickly without searching throughout the whole book. Turn to the index on page 48. Choose an entry, such as *fur,* and ask the child to use the index to find out how a moose's fur helps it stay warm. Repeat this exercise with as many entries as you like. Ask the child to point out the differences between an index and a glossary. (The index helps readers find information quickly, while the glossary tells readers what words mean.)

Where in the World?

Many plants and animals found in the Early Bird Nature Books series live in parts of the world other than the United States. Encourage the child to find the places mentioned in this book on a world map or globe. Take time to talk about climate, terrain, and how you might live in such places.

All the World in Metric!

Although our monetary system is in metric units (based on multiples of 10), the United States is one of the few countries in the world that does not use the metric system of measurement. Here are some conversion activities you and the child can do using a calculator:

WHEN YOU KNOW:	MULTIPLY BY:	TO FIND:
miles	1.609	kilometers
feet	0.3048	meters
inches	2.54	centimeters
gallons	3.787	liters
tons	0.907	metric tons
pounds	0.454	kilograms

Activities

Make up a story about moose. Be sure to include information from this book. Draw or paint pictures to illustrate your story.

Visit a zoo to see moose. How are moose like other deer at the zoo? How are they different? Do any of the moose have antlers? If so, are they shedding their velvet?

Act out being a moose. What do you do when an enemy is near? How do you get food and water? How do you stay warm in winter?

Glossary

antlers—bones that grow from the top of a male moose's head

bell—a flap of furry skin that hangs from a moose's throat

bull—a male moose

calves—baby moose

cast—fall off

cows—female moose

habitat—an area where a kind of animal can live and grow

herbivores (HUR-buh-vorz)—animals who eat only plants

hooves—a moose's feet

pedicle (PEH-dih-kuhl)—a soft, fuzzy spot on a male moose's head that grows into an antler

predators (PREH-duh-turz)—animals who hunt and eat other animals

ruminants (ROO-muh-nuhnts)—hoofed animals who usually have four stomachs

rut—the time in autumn when bull moose fight

velvet—soft, furry skin that protects antlers and helps them grow

Index